IMAGES
of America

AROUND PITTSFORD

Eaton Hall became the Pittsford Historical Society's office and museum when it was purchased from the Burlington Roman Catholic Diocese in 1981. Erected in 1877 by Otter Creek Masonic Lodge No. 70, it has since housed the first public high school, a boys' club, an elementary school, and the parish hall for St. Alphonsus Catholic Church. Mary Jane Eaton owned Eaton Hall from 1901 until 1924, when it was transferred from her estate to the three Pittsford churches. The Congregationalists and Methodists deeded their shares to the Roman Catholic Diocese of Burlington in 1962. It stood vacant from 1978 to 1981. (Photograph by John MacHardy.)

On the cover: Marion Chatterton (right), her little sister Ruth, and Tige pose across the village green from their home for photographer Mary T. Randall in 1910. The Congregational Church carriage sheds and burial ground are at left. The girls' father was hardware merchant Harley Mead Chatterton Jr. The recycled crate advertises Berry Brothers' varnish and wood finishes. (Author's collection.)

IMAGES
of America

AROUND PITTSFORD

Peggy Armitage
for Pittsford Historical Society Inc.

ARCADIA
PUBLISHING

Published by Arcadia Publishing
Charleston SC, Chicago IL, Portsmouth NH, San Francisco CA

Library of Congress Catalog Card Number: 2008930642

For all general information contact Arcadia Publishing at:
Telephone 843-853-2070
Fax 843-853-0044
E-mail sales@arcadiapublishing.com
For customer service and orders:
Toll-Free 1-888-313-2665

Visit us on the Internet at www.arcadiapublishing.com

*This book is dedicated to all who appreciate their heritage and preserve
their pictorial records for the enlightenment of all to come.*

CONTENTS

ACKNOWLEDGMENTS

Long before a small group of Pittsford natives founded the Pittsford Historical Society, I heard my elders' tales of our Mott and Rowley ancestors who settled here in the 1770s, their neighbors, and descendants. My great-great-aunt Helen Scofield Randall was nearing 90 when she told me about people she knew who lived in Fort Vengeance. Her daughter, Mary T. Randall Allen, taught me the names of ferns, wildflowers, and roses growing by the cellar holes of several early settlers.

I was among the group forming the historical society in 1960. Jane Belcher (first museum curator), Barbara Mericle, Alice Wimett, retired curator Jean Davies, and present curator Anne Pelkey laid the groundwork for this volume. Numerous old-timers, society members, and friends preserved Pittsford, Chittenden, and Proctor stories and images, making my task a very rewarding experience.

The following people and organizations provided information and many photographs never before published: Grant Adams, Elizabeth Atwood, Robert and Bonnie Baird, Ernest and Mary Lou Brod, John B. Cadwell, Camp Betsey Cox, Camp Sangamon, Chittenden and Proctor Historical Societies, Ernest Clerihew, Rebecca Davenport, retired town clerk Gordon DeLong, Ivy Dixon, Sarah L. Dopp, Richard Fifield, Nancy Gaudreau, Arthur Grace, Allen Hitchcock, Joseph and Laurie Kamuda, Nancy Kennedy, Barbara Ketcham, John MacHardy, Rebecca Mandolare, Helen Newton, Elinor Pike, Barbara Poljacik, Proctor librarian Mary Brough, Robert E. Pye, Louise Sanderson, Beth Saradarian, Katherine Sivret, Maclure librarian Bonnie Stewart, Peter and Dorothy Terwilliger, Dr. Margaret Waddington, Arthur Wardwell, Karen Webster, John and Linda Weeden, and Elmer and Frances Wheeler.

I am indebted to professional photographer Caleb Kenna of Brandon for loaning his light table to select images from Mary Allen's collection of glass plate negatives, and especially to Chris Wideawake, vice president of Phototec, for scanning them.

I am very grateful to Hilary Zusman, an Arcadia Publishing assistant editor, whose prompt and patient assistance was inspiring.

Unless otherwise noted, all images appear courtesy of the Pittsford Historical Society. Others appear courtesy of the Chittenden Historical Society (CHS), the Proctor Free Library/Proctor Historical Society (PFL/PHS), Sarah L. Dopp (SLD), and myself (author's collection).

INTRODUCTION

From the heights of land east and west of Otter Creek, the views of Pittsford, Proctor, and Chittenden may be as appealing today as they were to the militiamen on their way north in 1759 through the valley to do battle with French and Native American foes. Returning home on the Crown Point military road, the views from the top of the Great Falls in Pittsford, later named Sutherland Falls, would have been equally inviting.

One major difference in the old views would have been the giant trees stretching from the Taconic to Green Mountain peaks, with only glimpses of sunlight on the creek. Fertile valley soils, waterfalls, forested Green Mountains with beds of iron, and the huge marble deposits under the Taconics made a superb mix of natural resources to provide good lives for future settlers.

On October 12, 1761, Gov. Benning Wentworth of New Hampshire granted a tract of land west of the Connecticut River and six miles square to 63 proprietors, all of them investors in what would become Pittsford. Chittenden, organized in 1780, is named for Vermont's first governor. It covers the largest acreage in Rutland County. In 1887, a prosperous marble industry supported the community around Sutherland Falls. That year the state legislature created a separate town named for Redfield Proctor Sr., by then Vermont's governor and future U.S. senator. The new town encompassed portions of Pittsford and Rutland. Thus it was that a number of families went to bed in Rutland and Pittsford and woke up in Proctor.

The three towns have distinct physical features, but the residents have a great deal in common. They found husbands and wives and jobs in the adjoining towns and moved back and forth, sometimes moving their buildings or dismantling them to rebuild elsewhere. From the earliest years the same surnames appear everywhere: Barnard, Candon, Powers, Warner, Fox, Chatterton, Humphrey, Baird, Manley, Tarble, Randall, Hewitt, Ripley, Ladd, Mead, and more. When a plague of mosquitoes spread diseases in the 1800s, some Pittsford people moved to Chittenden's higher ground either temporarily or for good.

Farming was the chief occupation of the earliest arrivals. On his way home to Greenwich, Massachusetts, after the French and Indian War, Pittsford's first settler, Gideon Cooley, was determined to return and clear a piece of land near the foot of the Great Falls. He had made some improvements and a small shelter with the help of his brother Benjamin before buying the property in 1769 from an original proprietor, Col. Ephraim Doolittle. Doolittle was a land speculator and at one point owned about half the land in Pittsford.

The years leading up to the Revolution were perilous and slowed the influx of settlers. For one thing, land disputes between New Hampshire and New York made property ownership questionable. Once the war started, Tory sympathizers led small bands of Native Americans on raiding parties that burned crops and buildings and captured prisoners, carrying some off to

Canada. Fort Vengeance in Pittsford was one in a line of northernmost outposts beyond which the inhabitants could expect no protection by American military forces.

Farming continued as the chief occupation longer in Pittsford than in the other towns. In Pittsford Village there is now but one remaining farm, but as late as 1900 most residences on both sides of the village green were on small farms. Dairy farms flourished beginning in 1849 after the Burlington and Rutland Railroad tracks were laid. Shipping cast-iron stoves, butter, eggs, cheese, and other farm products by train was a major step forward, followed by the advent of refrigerated cars.

Among Chittenden's first settlers were Pittsford people. The lack of bottomland was made up for by the vast forests, which took years to reduce to lumber and charcoal. Sawmills, clapboard mills, gristmills, and blacksmith shops were soon clustered at the falls on Furnace Brook in Holden and along East Creek in South Chittenden, which was nicknamed Slab City in the 1900s. An 1869 map and directory of Chittenden lists nine sawmills, four clapboard mills, three gristmills, five blacksmith shops, one merchant/postmaster, one gunsmith, one listed as a farmer and blacksmith, one as "farmer and lumbering," and 24 farmers.

In the foothills of the Green Mountains, New Boston and Philadelphia were Chittenden hamlets populated by charcoal burners who produced tons of the product for smelting iron ore in the first Pittsford blast furnace on Furnace Flat, an area later named Grangerville.

From the time when marble was discovered in Pittsford and Proctor, farmers opened small quarries on their land. Most houses built in both towns from the early 1800s on have marble block foundations, while the few stone and brick buildings have marble door and window lintels.

Proctor began earning its reputation as the marble town with the opening of the Sutherland Falls quarry in 1838. That event was followed by the failure of small quarry owners lacking sound business judgment, mechanical know-how, and capital. Despite the 1849 arrival of rail service, a weak business climate slowed activity between 1845 and 1869, the year Rutland lawyer and Civil War veteran Redfield Proctor Sr. became the court-appointed receiver of the Dorr and Myers marble quarry.

Proctor historian David. C. Gale wrote in 1922 that when Colonel Proctor surveyed the scene, "he had a vision." He organized the Sutherland Falls Marble Company in 1870, moved to Proctor in 1871, and began buying out small business owners. Proctor, Vermont's governor in 1880, emerged as president of the new Vermont Marble Company.

By 1911, Governor Proctor's company owned the Rutland-Florence Marble Company's mill and thereafter bought Pittsford, Rutland, and West Rutland quarries. It acquired farms with promising marble deposits outright, or obtained rights to waters, to extract minerals and sand, and rights to dump sand from the mills' gang saws on spent lands.

Production branched out from sawing dimension marble to shaping architectural elements. With the dawn of the 20th century, European carvers and sculptors recruited by company officials arrived to start a highly successful department producing three-dimensional and high-relief figures. Sculptors and their carver helpers created the allegorical figures *Majesty of Law* and *Spirit of Justice* from two 85-ton blocks for the entrance to the Supreme Court building in Washington, D.C.

Vermont Marble Company was the largest employer in the area in 1961. After purchasing quarries in the United States and foreign countries, then president Mortimer Proctor wrote that from humble beginnings it grew to be the foremost marble company in the world.

Pluess-Staufer of Oftringen in Switzerland bought all of Vermont Marble Company's holdings in 1976 and closed all but the Vermont Marble Museum in 1993. Pluess-Staufer's Omya division now operates a major calcium carbonate plant in Florence, with offices in Proctor.

The Proctor family's beneficence is evident in Proctor and Pittsford public buildings still standing. Many more, long gone, are to be found in the images within this book.

Today Pittsford, Chittenden, and Proctor share the desirable qualities of small residential communities set in a rural Vermont landscape.

One

PEOPLE

The Taranovich family now owns Samuel Bassett Loveland's farm shown here on part of first settler Gideon Cooley's farm in Pittsford. Cooley's house was north of Sutherland Falls. Its shallow cellar hole is across the Proctor-Pittsford Road from Loveland's and marked by a sign. Since that remnant was plowed over for a garden the sign is now the only clue to Cooley's house site.

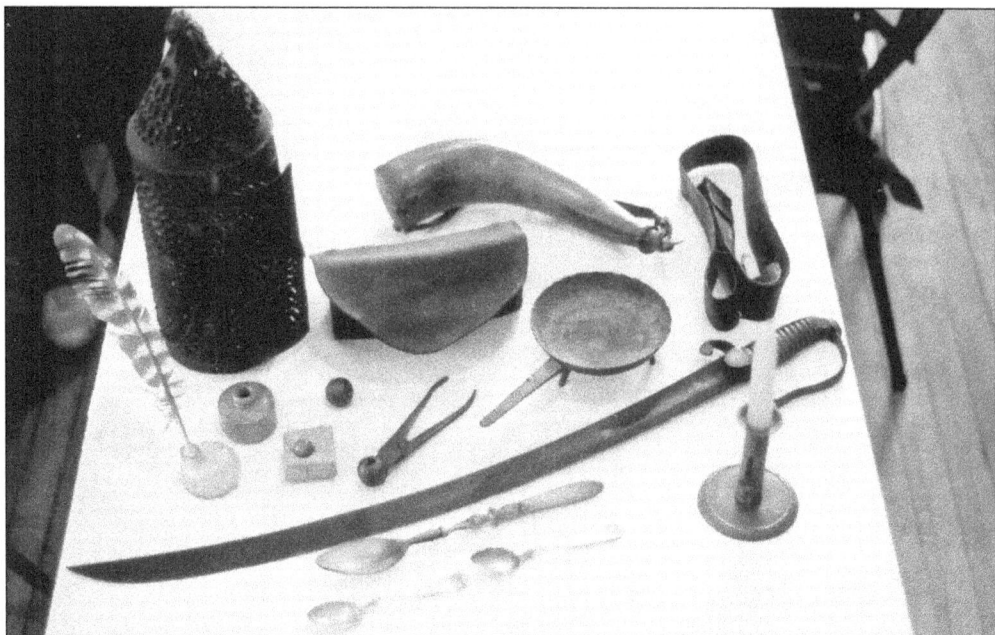

The possessions of the early Pittsford settlers were handed down through generations of their heirs. A few, now in the Pittsford Historical Museum, are shown clockwise from upper left: Revolutionary captain Benjamin Cooley's pierced tin lantern, cartridge case, powder horn, belt and sword, and glass and salt-glazed ink bottles. These surround two lead mini balls, Cooley's bullet mold, and an iron pan for melting lead. Below the sword are a tin candlestick, two coin silver teaspoons, and a large serving spoon, its bowl and handle made of cow horn. (Photograph by Clarence Holden.)

This photograph shows Caleb Hendee Jr.'s stoneware inkwell with Capt. John Mott's foot warmer and burl maple cup. Fort Mott, built around William and Beulah Cox's house in 1777, was named for him. It stood on the east bank of Otter Creek on the Holden farm now owned by Kelley and Thomas J. Turner. (Photograph by Clarence Holden.)

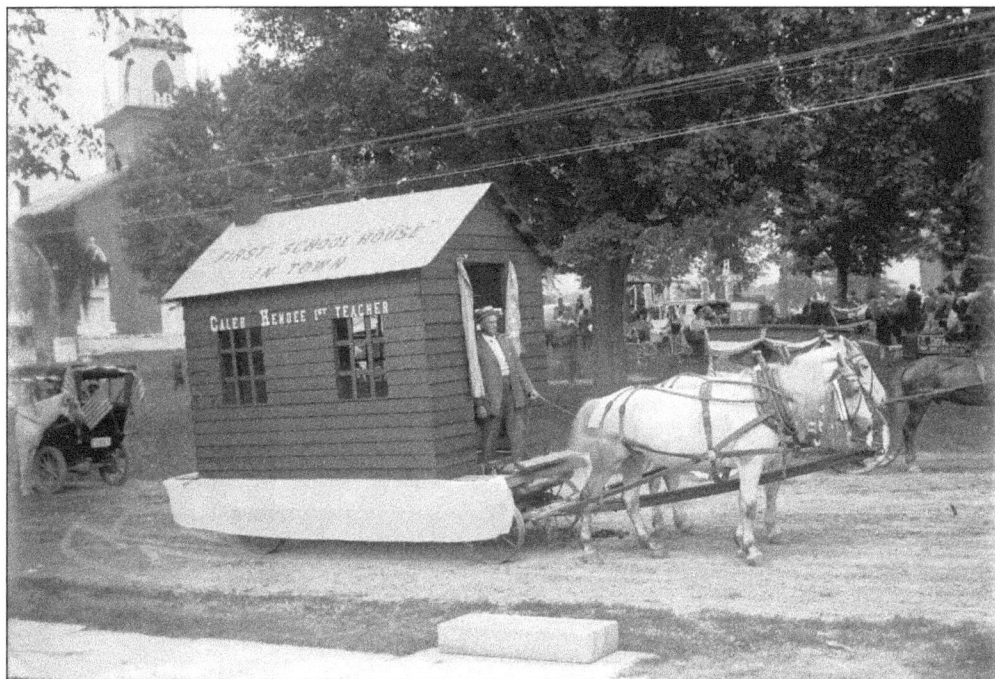

This 1911 float in the Pittsford charter's 150th anniversary parade honored Gen. Caleb Hendee Jr., the town's first schoolteacher and librarian, longtime town clerk, justice of the peace, Vermont surveyor general, and a general in the War of 1812. Hendee was 12 years old in 1780, when his parents' farm buildings were converted to Fort Vengeance, and his memoir describes its features in detail. (Photograph by Mary T. Randall.)

These 1911 parade units illustrate the transition from horse-drawn transportation to gasoline-powered automobiles. Similar celebrations still continue, including old home days, an Old English pageant, the U.S. bicentennial reenactment of a 1776 Congregational Church service, and annual state and national patriotic holidays. (Photograph by Mary T. Randall.)

11

Through the early 1900s, Pittsford musicians formed town bands. As their numbers dwindled, high school bands filled the gap. The Pittsford-Barstow High School Band fielded 18 musicians and a drum majorette. This photograph shows off the uniforms of a town band standing near Michael Connolly's tin shop on Main Street.

Pittsford organized parades with bands and floats celebrating old home days; historic anniversaries; laying cornerstones or dedicating monuments; famous sons, daughters, and war veterans; and dedicating the new water system and watering trough. Nickwackett Farm owner John B. Candon entered this power-driven butter churn in a parade marking the town's charter.

This float may have been inspired by James Fenimore Cooper's novel so named. Cooper was a popular 19th-century author in the northeast states, and his novels were set in the area. The float could also be intended to evoke the Native Americans who were numerous around Pittsford when the first settlers arrived.

The 1959 observance of Samuel de Champlain's discovery of the lake he named included no parade, but townspeople threw a weeklong party with a hobby show, an antiques show, a tourist information booth with maps of historic landmarks, and a Colonial-period pageant including these warriors. The finale was a fashion show closing in the dimmed hall with models dressed in antique nightwear, carrying lit candles, and singing "Good Night, Ladies."

In this modern version of *The Peaceable Kingdom*, Leslie Allen's Newfoundland and Grace and Helen Palmer's tiny terrier touch noses around 1920 with no apparent sign of a fight. Almost everyone in Pittsford kept pet and working dogs in their homes then as now. (Author's collection.)

The Rutland County Humane Society dedicated its new home (above) on Stevens Road in 1967. Cofounder Ellen Hollrock stands behind the speaker. Fourth from right is town manager Frank Anderson. The rest of the dignitaries represent the Rutland County area. Edward Wheeler's barn was the first shelter from the society's founding in 1959. A wing to house larger animals and a roof over the outdoor pens has since been added. (Courtesy of Beth Saradarian.)

Jocelyn Chutter is pictured in 1943. She is a daughter of Pittsford High School principal Col. Robert and Ruth Chutter, and married Emerson Frost in 1950, son of Dr. H. Leslie and Christine G. Frost. They live in the Chutter home and have continued their parents' service as pillars of the town. They both have been hospice volunteers; she is president of Evergreen Cemetery Association, and he is their church historian and former town zoning board member.

Dr. Henry Haven Swift was a highly regarded surgeon and photographer from the 1880s until his accidental death in 1926. He is seen here setting up a camera behind his roadster. That photography devotees went on picture-taking forays together is evident in this image, and by almost identical scenes found in several photographers' albums in the historical society's museum. Mount Nickwackett in Chittenden forms the backdrop.

Dr. John Baylor shows off his new car around 1900 for Grace Pinckney, John Willard Jr., and Sarsfield, Grace's Irish setter. Baylor came to Pittsford to be Dr. Henry Haven Swift's assistant. He and Grace were engaged to be married when he became ill and soon died. He was greatly mourned by all who knew him. (Author's collection.)

Jessie Hotchkiss married Dr. Harry Ross, who died in 1906. Their daughter Janet married Bradford Mead; together they developed the Pico Ski Area in Mendon. The Meads' daughter Andrea was the first American woman skier to win three gold medals in the Winter Olympics. (Author's collection.)

Dr. John I. Pinckney was Dr. Henry Haven Swift's assistant before he opened his own practice in Pittsford Village. He soon became assistant to Dr. Henry Dexter Chadwick, first medical director of the Pittsford Sanatorium for tuberculosis patients. Pinckney went on to head a sanatorium in Rutland, Massachusetts, and another in Greenwood Mountain, Maine. He died in 1948 after 25 years as director of the Providence Tuberculosis League in Rhode Island. (Author's collection.)

This tavern in Pittsford Village was built by James Ewings in 1795. Ebenezer Blanchard Rand was proprietor until 1851. His son Egbert Blanchard Rand sold the property in 1892 to a cousin, John M. Goodnough, who added the high-style exterior touches. Goodnough's daughter Grace married Charles Pinckney. From left, the figures are Goodnough's wife and Grace G. Pinckney with her children, Gertrude, John I., Jessie, and Grace.

Dr. George B. Armington practiced medicine in Providence, Rhode Island, before coming to Pittsford; Charles D. Brown, son of Brown the tanner, married the doctor's daughter Jane Armington in 1849. Jane and her daughter Harriet B. Day were two of "the Providence ladies," as they were called, who spent summers at the Otter Creek Inn. They are pictured during a stay in Pittsford. (Author's collection.)

From left to right, George Hendee and brothers William and Warren and their terrier enjoyed a typical day's catch of native trout on one of Pittsford's famous streams around 1900. They came from a long line of hunters and fishermen descended from early settler Deacon Caleb Hendee Sr. and his son, Gen. Caleb Hendee Jr. Some 54 years later, Pres. Dwight Eisenhower was invited to stay at Mountain Top Inn in Chittenden for a few days and to try his luck at fishing Furnace Brook. Someone had thoughtfully sprayed the brook for mosquitoes, but it also killed the insects that trout feed on. The president hardly got a rise. (Author's collection.)

From left to right, Hazel Leonard, Elinor Pike, and Louise Willis playfully display a less-than-record-breaking catch in the 1960s. However, a *Rutland Herald* reporter states that Pike landed a 34-inch rainbow trout weighing three and a half pounds. The fourth member of this group was Jane Belcher, daughter of Stephen P. Belcher II, who invented the famous dry fly that Jane named Spirit of Pittsford Mills.

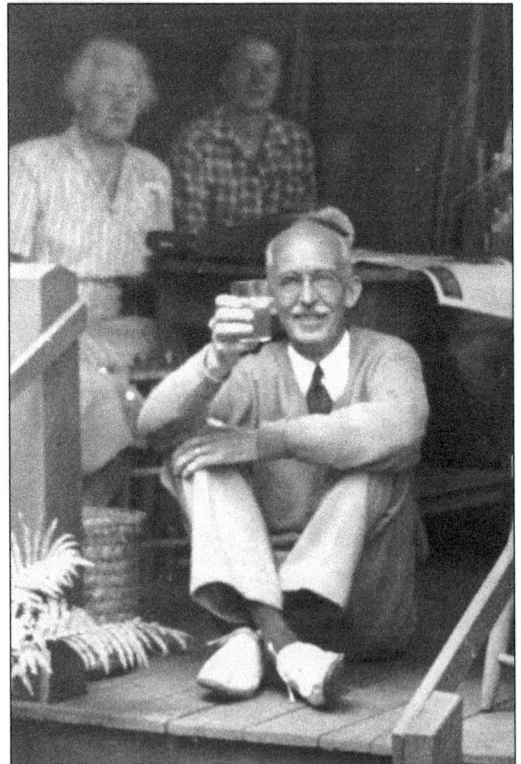

Stephen P. Belcher II lifts a toast to his son, Stephen P. III, stationed in Africa in World War II. In the porch shadows are Jane and her mother, Margaret Colburn Belcher, daughter of Charles S. Colburn, Esq. He practiced law in the 1870s and later served as town clerk, judge of Rutland Probate Court, and state senator. His office became home to Dr. Swift's daughter, Katherine Swift Frazier.

Mary T. Randall was listed as a commercial photographer in *Walton's Register* of Vermont business owners from 1907 to 1909. She studied photography and graduated from the University of Vermont. This is her graduation picture. After she married Leslie Allen in 1918, they lived in her parents' brick house in the village until Mary sold the house and outbuildings to Harold and Lois Blittersdorf. Under Mary's guidance, Leslie became a fine photographer.

Mary T. Randall's parents were Helen Scofield Randall and Julius S. Randall. Helen Randall, born in 1848, often retold stories she heard from early settlers' children who had lived through the Revolutionary War near Fort Vengeance. Here she stands by her hydrangea around 1915. She died at age 91, her memory still intact. (Author's collection.)

May E. Manley was also listed in *Walton's Register*. Born in 1861, she is about 45 in this self-portrait. Her home studio was in Pittsford Mills until she moved to upper Arch Street. She specialized in portraiture; her studio props included a fur rug and fancy wicker furniture. A "modern woman," she drove a Stanley Steamer and served on the boards of several corporations.

Agnes Mulligan Keith was one of three Mulligan sisters who married three Keith brothers. Her portrait reveals the telltale fur rug in Manley's self-portrait. Agnes and Francis Keith had two girls and seven boys; the boys became successful business owners in town, and several of their offspring now conduct thriving Pittsford businesses.

In the latter half of the 1800s, farm families often posed with favorite horses for itinerant photographers. At least three generations of Michael Carrigan's family posed with their horses about 1870 in front of the homestead on Adams Road. Michael's parents came to Pittsford from Ireland. The Carrigan men worked at the furnace; some married furnace workers' daughters.

Elbert William Eayres's family lived on this farm on the road to Rutland. It still stands, minus the porches, opposite Theodore Burditt's Maple Shade Farm (now Winslow's). The last of the Eayres descendants living here were Robert E. and Elizabeth Moodie Degenhardt's children. The scene dates from the late 1800s.

Elbert William Eayres married Pawlet schoolteacher Sarah Greene, shown in her elaborately fashioned wedding dress, the sleeves trimmed with lace. Her heirs gave her hand-stitched quilt to the Shelburne Museum. The quilt and the home where she pieced it are in the museum's book about its outstanding collection of quilts. (Courtesy of Rebecca Degenhardt Mandolare.)

This picture shows a group in 1933 reenacting a pioneering moment next to the Eayres maple grove. On horseback is Theodore Burditt, with Suzie Morseman and "Laddie" in the covered wagon. Standing from left to right are Sarah Greene "Grandma" Eayres, Dorothy Burditt, Cora Wheeler, Alphonse Langlois, and Mr. Goss. The seated lady with a banjo is identified as Mrs. Shedrick. Mrs. Goss sits beside her. (Courtesy of Rebecca Degenhardt Mandolare.)

Much later in life, Sarah Greene Eayres's aged, always thrifty husband was still recycling mountains of burlap bags that came with sheep and horse feed in them; he patiently wound the ravelings into these giant balls of twine. (Courtesy of Rebecca Degenhardt Mandolare.)

Cabinetmaker George D. Bates's family lived in this house on Corn Hill Road. Bates's grandparents Joshua and Rebecca Bates bought it in 1801. It burned in 1974. Four generations of Bates men were skillful woodworkers. George D. built the Maclure Library book stacks and librarian's station. His son Douglas Bates turned lamp bases and four-poster beds.

The Otter Creek Inn, known by 1920 as the "old hotel," burned to the ground in 1931. The lot remained empty until Joseph S. and Josephine Kamuda built their general store in 1939. Josephine ran the store alone while Joseph was in World War II. This picture of them dates from about 1950. Their son Joseph J. and his wife Laureen now run the business as Kamuda's Country Market. (Courtesy of Joseph and Laureen Kamuda.)

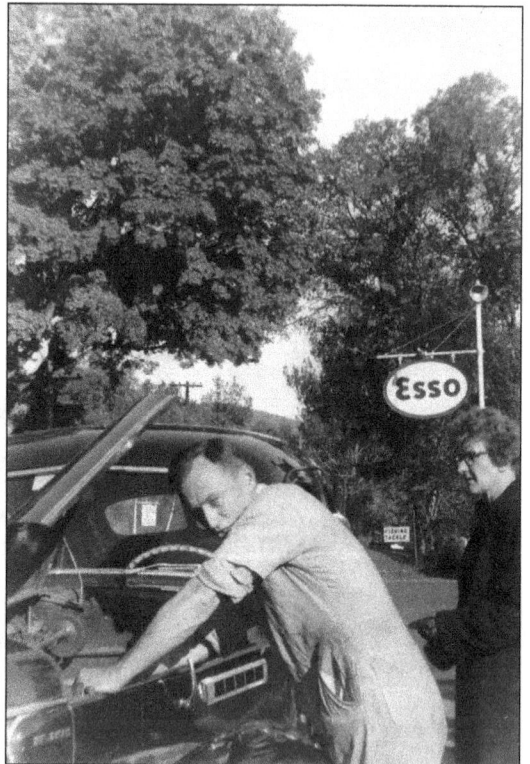

George Terwilliger took over the Esso station in the village after he, his brother Jack, and their wives sold Rolling Acres Inn (now Telemark Ski Club) across Route 7 from the station. Here George works under the hood of Elizabeth Roberts's Desoto while she waits. (Courtesy of Dorothy and Peter Terwilliger.)

Terwilliger (left) holds a red fox while hunting partner and author Harold Blaisdell prepares to skin it. A similar scene illustrates one of many magazine articles he wrote for *Fur-Fish-Game*, *True*, *Argosy*, and *Vermont Life*. His first sale paid him $6. His first of four books was *Tricks That Take Fish*. Blaisdell designed programs and taught physically ill and handicapped children at the Caverly Child Health Center in Pittsford for 17 years. (Courtesy of Dorothy and Peter Terwilliger.)

Fires consumed many Pittsford homes, barns, mills, and acres of woodlands. George Terwilliger (center) confers with National Guardsmen during a forest fire that spread underground in 1953 on Fire Hill in Florence. Drought conditions and tinder-dry earth occupied hundreds of firefighters and equipment, tents, food, and cooks for weeks. The scar is still visible. (Courtesy of Dorothy and Peter Terwilliger.)

Terwilliger died soon after the Florence forest fire burned out in late 1953. His son Peter left college to run the business for 28 years. In this picture of Pittsford High School's 1951–1952 baseball team, Peter (center) gleefully sticks out his tongue at the end of a perfect 12-0 season with a Marble Valley League championship. (Courtesy of Dorothy and Peter Terwilliger.)

From left to right, Jane Dow, Dorothy Sanderson, and Mary Powers were schoolmates in this 1940 picture. Sanderson married Peter Terwilliger and coached Girl Scout skiers, supervised the Recreation Area swimming program, and sang in the Congregational Church choir. Peter has been a volunteer fireman, school board member, board member of First National Bank of Brandon, and a bird-hunting guide. (Courtesy of Peter and Dorothy Terwilliger.)

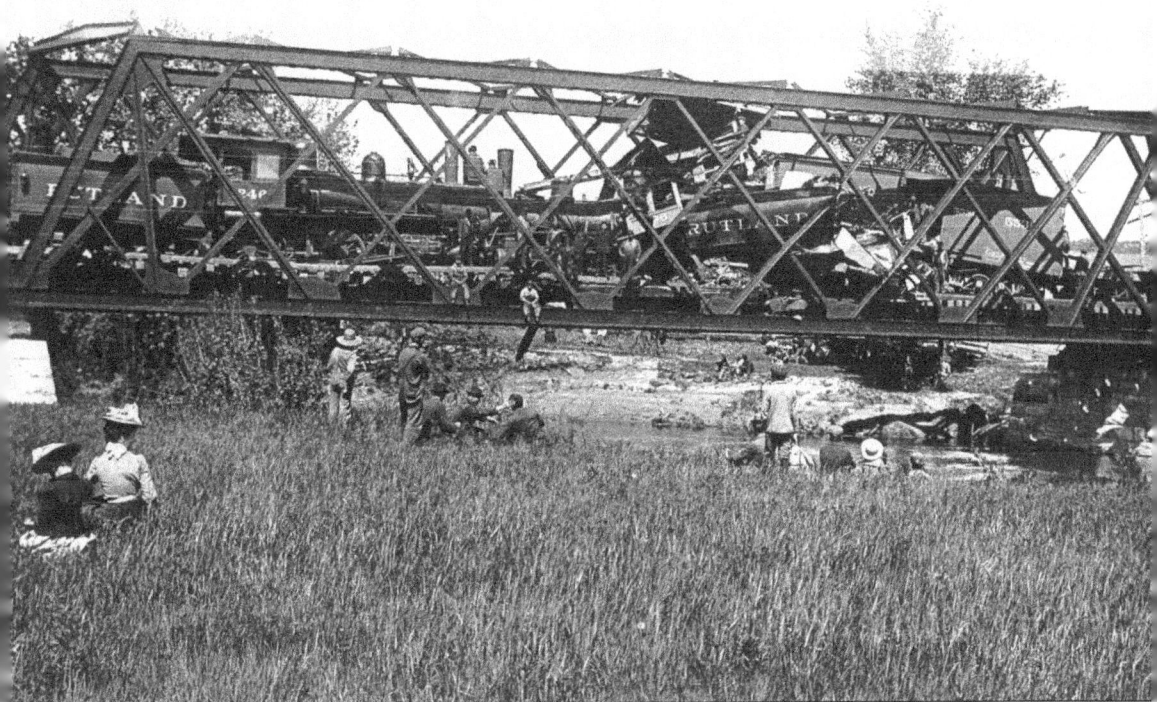

Rail disasters were exciting but infrequent diversions. A freight train struck Pittsford's depot in 1895; the resulting fire destroyed it. A mile south, a passenger train broke through the wooden railway bridge. These picnickers watch trains being untangled in the bridge south of the Florence station in 1902. Another train hit a 4,000-gallon milk tanker crossing the Florence track in 1957. The truck's cab shoved the station four inches west. No one died or suffered serious injuries in these accidents. Nor did anyone while William B. Shaw's barn at Pittsford Mills burned in 1889, but watching fires was a recreational pastime when the 1901 fire wiped out the factories and mills along Furnace Brook, next to Shaw's store.

Less exciting but more fun to watch is this red-hot 1904 croquet game on William B. Shaw's lawn.

Abundant pictures of picnics suggest that some people spent most of the summer picnicking. This outing took place at Amos Tiffany's grove and spring north of Pinewoods Road. Hatted and seated second from left is Dr. Henry Haven Swift; Harry Winter lounges in front of him. The grande dame atop the table is unidentified. Seated behind the table are Leslie and Mary R. Allen, and next to them are Florence Palmer Winter and her sister Grace Palmer. (Author's collection.)

Around 1910, these period-costumed ladies play whist in Cora Belle Pinckney's parlor. Her back is to the camera, her luxuriant brown hair piled high. Fourth from the left is Dr. Chadwick's wife. Betsey Penfield Manley is seated fifth from left.

Jane Pinckney (she changed her given name shortly after marrying) shocked many of her friends and the doctor's patients by wearing men's knickers and sneakers and smoking cigarettes at this hunting camp on Bee Brook in Chittenden. (Her hair is properly coiffed.) From the 1920s on, she drove the doctor everywhere in her Packards. He never bothered to learn how. (Author's collection.)

Snowshoeing was the rage in the early 1900s. Mary T. Randall joined parties of 10 and more bundled in heavy wool skirts, trousers, sweaters, hats, and mittens. Someone got this shot of her with King. He belonged to Dr. Henry Dexter Chadwick, first medical director of the Vermont Sanatorium. Dr. Chadwick held the position from late 1907 to 1913, which dates this picture from those years. (Author's collection.)

These hardy hikers pose in the Pinckney family's rustic Brookside Camp on Furnace Brook. The walls were papered with white birch bark. Seated at far left is Grace Goodnough Pinckney. Standing third from left is Edith Nichols Chadwick; wearing a fur hat in that row is Dr. Chadwick. Mary T. Randall stands at far right. (Author's collection.)

The Nature Club kept records of flora and fauna discovered all over town, listed by common and Latin names and where, when, and by whom found. As shown here, they were well prepared with lunch containers and equipment, which included field glasses and plant presses to examine and preserve specimens. Mary T. Randall is third from left in the back row. (Author's collection.)

Royal W. Barnard was born in Chittenden and moved to Pittsford around 1898. His daughter Mary Barnard Monroe became a milliner with a shop in Brandon but later returned to Pittsford. She is seen at left around 1900, presumably modeling one of her own hats. The other lady is unidentified; perhaps she is a customer wearing one of Monroe's hats. (Courtesy of Ivy Anderson Dixon.)

In this photograph, young Reginald Barnard stands by his curious vehicle about 1911 at the home of his grandparents, Royal W. and Helen T. Barnard. Below, his cousin Gladys Whitney shows off her first car in 1915. She was brought up by her Barnard grandparents and married George W. Neil in 1917. They lived out their lives in the Barnard house. She sang in the Methodist Church choir on Sundays and on many other occasions. Neil represented Pittsford in the Vermont legislature from 1939 to 1961. (Below, courtesy of Ivy Anderson Dixon.)

The Neils' daughter Grace married Frank Anderson in 1945. He was home from Europe before heading to the Pacific. The attack on Hiroshima canceled his assignment. Grace wrote *In the Shadow of Cox Mountain* and *Betsey Cox: First Generation Vermonter* for young adults. (Courtesy of Ivy Anderson Dixon.)

Five generations of Barnards have owned the Barnard Funeral Home since 1898. From left to right are J. Hilton Barnard, his wife Mary, and children John H. (better known as "Jake") and Doris. Father and son operated the business from 1943 to 1995. John H. Barnard was a founding member and chief of the Pittsford Volunteer Fire Department. His son David Barnard is the fifth funeral director. (Courtesy of Ivy Anderson Dixon.)

Mrs. Dragon's first graders are shown at Eaton Hall, reopened in 1957 for overflow Lothrop School students. From left to right are (first row) Mary Patch, Edward Eugair, and unidentified; (second row) Peter Armitage, unidentified, Jacqueline Barnard, James Keith, Robert White, and Michael Pinkham; (third row) Robert Hemple, Shelly Fillioe, Jan ?, Ivy Anderson, and Nancy Hathaway. (Courtesy of Ivy Anderson Dixon.)

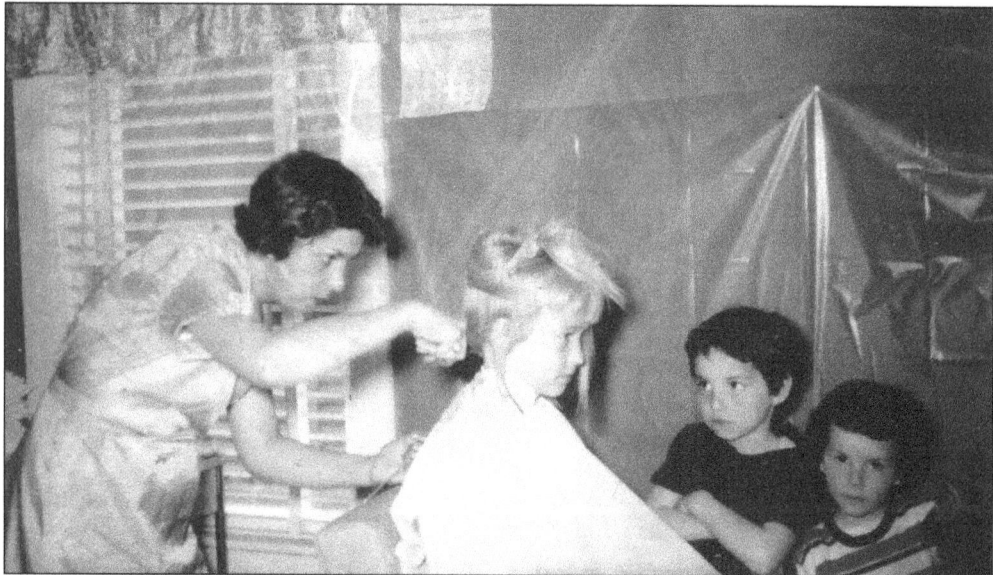

Josephine Margo married Edward F. Keith Sr. in 1950. She operated Joey's Beauty Shop in their village home from then until retiring in the late 1990s. People still recall it as a meeting place for the neighborhood women. She was a Girl Scout leader for many years. In this 1959 scene, Keith gives Ivy Anderson an annual summer pixie haircut. Margo and Joan Keith await their turns. (Courtesy of Ivy Anderson Dixon.)

From 1938 to 1986, Sarah Hooker Hendee, affectionately known as "Aunt Sallie," and her daughter Elizabeth cared for hundreds of foster children from infants to late teens in their home on Plains Road. Elizabeth also drove her own school bus. Sarah Hendee is shown in an uncommonly quiet moment at home. (Courtesy of Ivy Anderson Dixon.)

In 1922, Leone and Eleanor Smith, shown with David (left) and James, founded Camp Sangamon for boys. The Smiths came to Pittsford in 1916. He was formerly director of Mary Jane Eaton's Boys Club. Still family owned and operated, Camp Sangamon's swimming, boating, and fishing programs take place on the small farm where boys learn to use farm tools in gardening and caring for livestock. (Courtesy of Camp Sangamon.)

Charles and Jean Smith Davies launched Camp Betsey Cox for girls in 1953. This photograph of the first-year staff and campers shows Jean Davies holding Sherry in the second row. Charles sits right of them, with elder daughter Joanne sitting in a counselor's lap. Jean and Charles retired in 1989. At left in the first row is their niece and current camp director Lorrie Smith Byrom. (Courtesy of Camp Betsey Cox.)

Fred Harvie was Eaton Hall's head of buildings and grounds for 25 years. The Harvies came to Pittsford in 1974. Jean is an ardent genealogist; he was a well-known builder of dollhouses. They opened Fred's Dollhouse and Miniatures in 1980. Jean was the historical society treasurer for 24 years. Fred is shown in Eaton Hall. He and other volunteers transformed a vacant building to an outstanding history museum.

Ernest Clerihew is an antique car enthusiast (and schoolteacher and board member of the Pittsford Historical Society) who makes public events more fun for everyone, especially those invited to go for a spin with him. He is parked in a 1914 Ford Model T, one of several models he owns, in front of the Maclure Library during its 100th anniversary.

Violet Frett (left) and Lois Blittersdorf sell historical society sweatshirts at a fund-raiser during the 1976 bicentennial. They were active society members and cochaired the membership committee. Blittersdorf, a real estate broker, was president and listed the Village Green National Historic District. Her husband owned Vermont Art Studio. Frett's husband was a fine cabinetmaker.

41

This house on Furnace Road was reserved for middle-management employees of the Grangers who owned the iron furnace in the mid-1800s. Head teamster John Matthews may be the man in a bowler seated at left. Foundry boss Richard Mooney lived next door. The front porch remains unaltered. Town clerk Wilfred Cassidy owned the house for over 20 years. Town recreation director Randal Adams is the present owner.

Pittsford and Chittenden people cherish Furnace Brook for its trout waters. Dr. John I. Pinckney's Brookside Camp in Chittenden was the 1909 site of Margaret Colburn's marriage to Stephen P. Belcher II. The *Rutland Herald* noted that "The interior was draped with maiden hair ferns and daisies and the bridge and piazza were festooned with green vines and yellow primroses." (Author's collection.)

Above Brookside Camp, the Swifts hosted trout breakfasts and birthdays at their camp. This group gathered in 1919 for Katherine Swift Frazier's birthday. Third from left is Martha Wood Belcher, who would be feted here at her 76th party in 1920. Her daughter Hilda is seated at far right. She was a nationally recognized portrait artist. Collectors also prize Martha's oil and watercolor landscapes to this day. (Author's collection.)

Fred McGee is courting Orissa Libby in this buggy on the tree-shaded country lane pictured here around 1900. The courtship continued until Fred successfully completed his aim to marry his sweetheart. It is said that the couple lived happily for many years in Chittenden. (Courtesy of CHS.)

Timothy Cheedle, shown with his family about 1875, had a sawmill on Furnace Brook in Holden Village, across the brook from what is now the U.S. Fish Hatchery. Cheedle sold six acres of land halfway up Cheedle Hill, now Stoney Hill Road, to the Congregational Church. The church they built was last used as a Grange hall. It will soon become home to the Chittenden Historical Society. (Courtesy of CHS.)

River Road follows Furnace Brook north out of Holden to the Morgan horse farm owned in the 1960s by Dr. Frank and Margaret Lathrop. They bought the Orlovski farm, named it Furnace Brook Morgan Horse Farm, and raised prize-winning Morgans. Here the Lathrops enjoy a snowy sleigh ride behind one of theirs. (Courtesy of Katherine Sivret.)

Edgar Sivret Sr. drives a team of Morgans and guests past the Lathrop barn. He came with the stallion Orland Bold Admiral to Chittenden from Green Mountain Stock Farm in Randolph to work for the Lathrops. (Courtesy of Katherine Sivret.)

Edgar Sivret Sr. and Orland Bold Admiral performed a high-stepping routine in 1971 at one of many Vermont horse shows they attended. Sivret died much too young in a freak accident. Edgar Jr., who had worked with his father, took his place at the farm. After her husband's death Katherine Sivret continued to help the Lathrops with haying and other farm chores. Dr. Margaret Waddington now owns the Lathrop farm. She is an accomplished author and illustrates her books about living in Chittenden with her own photographs. (Courtesy of Katherine Sivret.)

Merritt Wheeler grew up in North Chittenden. The Wheelers lived on West Road in this old house, thought by some to belong to a Churchill and long since gone. Merritt Wheeler stands second from left with his brother Floyd at right. The Wheeler farm has descended through the Wheeler, Breed, and Parker families. The current owners are David and Michelle Parker. (Courtesy of Bonnie and Robert Baird.)

In this 1978 image, Merritt Wheeler heads out on a racing sulky with his Morgan horse for a drive on Chittenden's unpaved roads. By the time this picture was taken he had moved his family down from North Chittenden to their own farm on the River Road in Holden. Wheeler was road commissioner for many years. (Courtesy of Bonnie and Robert Baird.)

Robert and Bonnie Pomainville Baird began farming the Ralph O. and Sara Baird farm in North Chittenden when they married in 1976. A Pittsford farm girl, she grew up on the Pomainville farm, now Thor and Virginia Konwin's Branford House Antiques. Robert Baird stands in a barn doorway at their farm. His mother, Sara Wetmore Baird, "took summer people" from the 1930s to 1960, calling it Valley View Farm Guest House. (Courtesy of Robert and Bonnie Baird.)

Ralph O. Baird's widow Sara eventually lost her sight but easily got around the house and remained active. Here she is at home still able to crochet an afghan. The younger Bairds renamed the place Baird Farm after her death.

Robert and Bonnie Baird ran the dairy farm on West Road until they sold the herd and began raising newborn heifer calves to be shipped before they calved to buyers in distance places, including the Middle East. They converted the maple-gathering process from sap buckets to gravity-fed tubing first, then to a mechanical extraction system. This is their view to the southwest, with the Taconic mountains on the horizon. (Courtesy of Robert and Bonnie Baird.)

In this picture dated 1906, Aaron Congdon balances on a fence with his shotgun and the duck he bagged. His father owned a sawmill on East Creek by the road leading from South Chittenden to the Chittenden Reservoir, which is what many still call the Big Dam. (The East Pittsford dam was called the Little Dam.) Aaron's father or another Congdon ran C. Reed Holden's steam sawmill far up on Bloodroot Mountain. (Courtesy of CHS.)

In 1976, Gov. Richard Snelling listened to Agnes Rollins Gould, dressed in early American style, read her poem commemorating the nation's bicentennial on the front steps of the Frederic Duclos Barstow Memorial School. At 100 years of age in 1983, Gould became the oldest Chittenden resident. Elizabeth Baird (right) also enjoyed the moment. (Courtesy of Robert and Bonnie Baird.)

Frederic Duclos Barstow was the only son of William Slocum Barstow and Francoise Duclos Barstow. Their home was in South Chittenden and has since been an inn off and on in recent years. Born in 1895, Frederic Barstow died at age 36 in 1931. In his memory his parents built the Barstow School in 1933 on the road from East Pittsford into South Chittenden and gave it to the town. (Courtesy of CHS.)

Freeman Baird poses with his shotgun and hunting dog about 1880. He was a Civil War veteran and one of David Baird Sr.'s 12 children. He probably was 65 years old in this picture. His father owned a sawmill on East Creek in South Chittenden. Except for gunsmith Stephen Baird, whose home and gun shop still stand opposite Sangamon Road in South Chittenden, the Bairds were farmers or sawyers scattered throughout town. (Courtesy of CHS.)

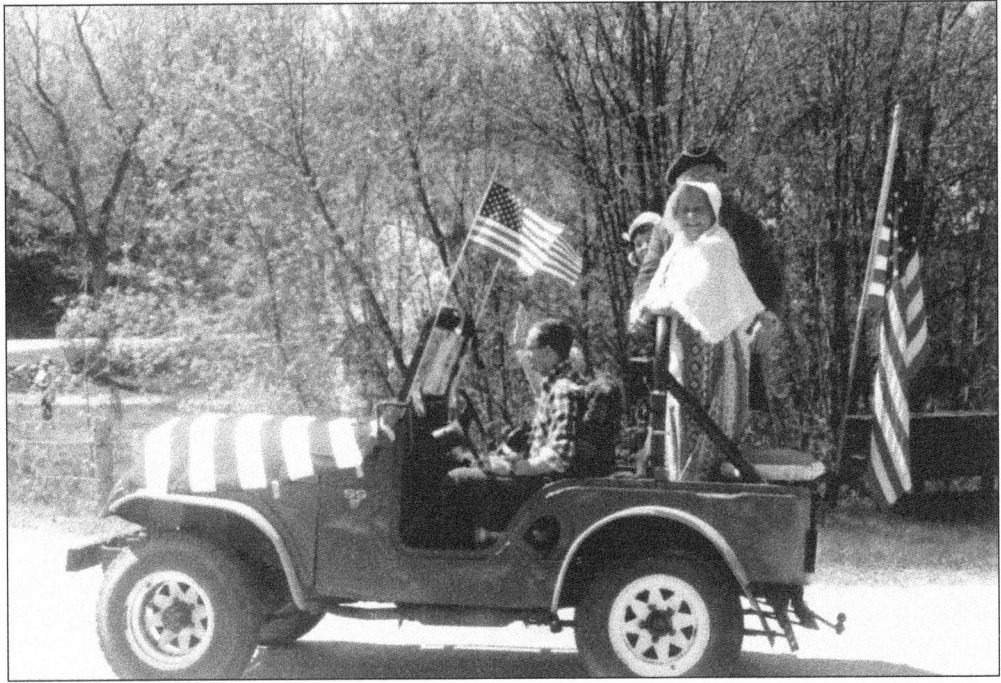

Chittenden celebrated July Fourth in 1981 with a parade that included a flag-bedecked Jeep. The driver is unidentified. The woman wearing a white shawl is Elizabeth Baird. Behind her is Robert Bearor in a tricorn hat, and Amy Taylor in a white bonnet peeks around him. They may have been portraying the George Washington family. (Courtesy of Robert and Bonnie Baird.)

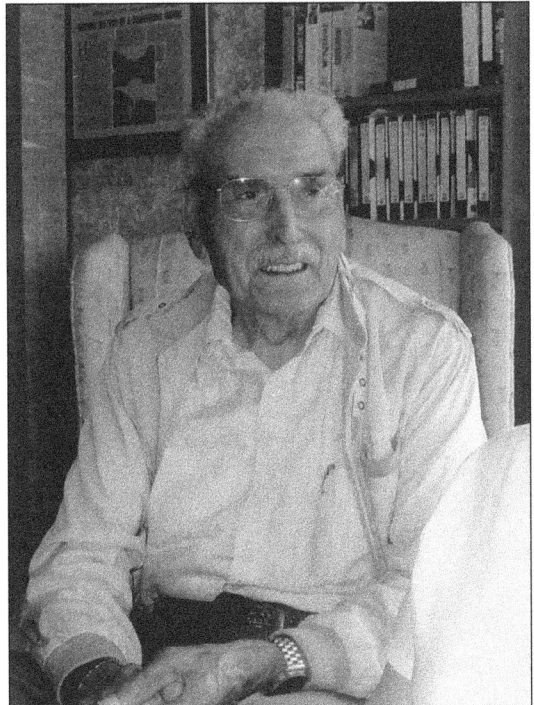

Arthur Wardwell was 98 in this picture. He was born and still summers on the Hibbard/Atwood farm on Wildcat Road. He walked to School No. 8, built by Loren Atwood about 1868 and later to Pittsford High School, boarding with nearby families and hiking back home Friday nights. He graduated Phi Beta Kappa from the University of Vermont. His U.S. Coastal Geodetic Survey, U.S. Navy, and research vessel captain's careers took him around the world. (Courtesy of Elizabeth Atwood.)

Arthur Wardwell's Atwood relatives gathered in 1953 on the porch of the old grade school, now named Lorenwood. Frances Atwood Wing is sitting behind her nieces Barbara Atwood Pratt (left) and Barbara's sister Elizabeth, with young James Pratt on her lap. She is a retired hand weaver and teacher and lives in Proctor. (Courtesy of Elizabeth Atwood.)

The names of these Chittenden Independent Band members have been forgotten, but their uniforms resemble those worn by the Pittsford band. The one exception is the sergeant kneeling at right in a uniform that suggests the photograph was taken sometime after the Civil War. (Courtesy of CHS.)

This brand-new automobile is identified only as "Austin's car," and one of the young ladies is Rhea (Horton) Meade. Judging from the features of the car with its wooden wheel spokes, windshield, and convertible canvas top, the picture could have been taken around 1925. The style of the women's clothing and hair suggests that date as well. (Courtesy of CHS.)

Kelley Holden and Thomas J. Turner were married in 1985. Their wedding reception was held in Pittsford's old town hall, built in 1912 and now the Lothrop Elementary School gymnasium and cafeteria. The bride dances in the gown she made with a beaded bodice trimmed with lace. Her dancing partner is Newton Wetmore, whose lifelong home is in North Chittenden. (Courtesy of Robert and Bonnie Baird.)

Proctor had two excellent photographers from the late 1800s into the 1900s. Jessie Warner Eckley, shown here setting up her camera around 1894, was known as a professional town photographer. Her parents, born in Pittsford, moved to Proctor. She recorded Proctor people and scenes in about equal numbers, whereas the Vermont Marble Company employed a professional to record company personnel and interior and exterior views of company property. (Courtesy of SLD.)

Jessie Eckley's granddaughter Sarah L. Dopp now owns Eckley's photographs. The collection contains images of Proctor people and sites other than her own. This 1870s view of Miss Steele's students on the North School steps includes Jessie, but the children are randomly identified, making it impossible many years later to spot her. (Courtesy of SLD.)

The George Davis (left) and Fletcher Proctor homes rise in the distance above these men laying water pipes across Otter Creek and under South Street around 1900. Young marble company workers dug the ditch by hand from springs on Mount Nickwackett in Chittenden down Adams and Corn Hill Roads in Pittsford into Proctor Village. Patrick Mooney from Pittsford was boss of the diggers. He said they received bonuses for finishing the job before the ground froze. (Courtesy of SLD.)

Albert Parmalee Humphrey directed the Proctor Band for many years. Elderly residents recall other town bands, one of them made up of Italian men who helped build the Chittenden Reservoir dam. Humphrey's ancestors were Joseph and Hannah Parmalee Humphrey. (Courtesy of SLD.)

Sadie Humphrey is seated on the lower step of the Humphrey brick house, now gone, on West Street. One of the women behind her is identified as Lillie Gibbs. Humphrey was an accountant for the Vermont Marble Company and later served many more years as town clerk of Proctor. The first Humphrey settler was Joseph Humphrey, who came from Winchester, New Hampshire, in 1784 and married Hannah Parmalee of Pittsford about 1795. Their son William built this house in 1826. The Humphreys opened a commercial marble quarry east of the house in 1836. (Courtesy of SLD.)

Maggie (left) and Magda Morganson, daughters of Peter Morganson, are dressed in their best for a picture-taking session, presumably on the steps of the home farm on the east side of South Street and south of the Fletcher Proctor residence. It is known that the Morgansons lived in Myron C. Warner's house, south of the marble bridge and on Otter Creek's west bank, until he completed construction on their new house. (Courtesy of SLD.)

These boys are identified as Peter and Frankie Morganson, brothers of the two girls above. Similar window sashes in these two pictures suggest that they are all standing outside the same house. It may be the same house Myron Warner built for the Morgansons. (Courtesy of SLD.)

Grace Noyes is identified in Jessie Warner Eckley's handwriting, "on the lawn of Myron Warner's house August 26, 1895." The chain on her bicycle has a guard, but one wonders if she avoided catching her skirt in it, or for that matter the wheel spokes. The old covered bridge above Sutherland Falls is partially hidden at left by the trees. The George Davis house rises over all. (Courtesy of SLD.)

In the same setting as that of Noyes's image, this photograph of two little Proctor sisters identifies them as Margaret (left) and Dorothy Chisholm. Although not at the same time, they both married Mortimer Proctor. Jessie Eckley's shrubs and flower beds appear often at the same stage of bloom in her works so that undated images can be estimated. (Courtesy of SLD.)

Eckley's portrait titled "Mr. Moore's Family" is dated August 10, 1895. Although they are listed as Etta, George, Florence, Gertrude, Arthur, Robert, Charles, Harry, Edgar, Mabel, and Marguerite on the reverse, they are not individually identified. Probably the parents are seated at far left and far right. A Moore family, perhaps this one, once lived on Green Square. (Courtesy of SLD.)

In 1880, Sen. Redfield Proctor merged his marble businesses into one company, the Vermont Marble Company. In this 1904 image he is 73, retired from his position as company president, and fishing on the Tobique River in New Brunswick, Canada. The Tobique Fishing Club maintained a camp there for members to relax and enjoy salmon fishing. Fletcher Proctor succeeded his father as president. Frank Partridge served from 1911 to 1935, followed by Redfield Proctor Jr. (Courtesy of PFL/PHS.)

Chicago

These Proctor Marble Company officials visited the 1893 World's Columbian Exposition in Chicago, where this photograph would have been taken. Listed from left to right are (first row) Guy H. Boyce, Bernie Robinson, and Ned Norton; (second row) Ned Arnold, Bert Dodge, ? Slack, and Will Donahue. The heads of their canes are capped with brass alligators, perhaps fair souvenirs or symbols of fraternal or other groups. (Courtesy of PFL/PHS.)

Aristide J. Piccini represents the Italian sculptors recruited in the first half of the 1900s. Born in 1883, Piccini worked with sculptors Tamante Ambrosini, his sons Dino and Derno, Orfeo Mutti, Renzo Palmerini, and more who created famous monuments and figures, heroic statues, and decorative ornamentation for public and private sites in America and abroad. Other sculptors, carvers, and stoneworkers were Polish, Czech, Swedish, Hungarian, and Irish immigrants. Locally their work can be found in churches, cemeteries, and the Vermont Marble Museum. They produced the marble columns in the rotunda at the National Art Gallery in Washington, D.C. In the 1970s, some of these men found work at Gawet Marble and Granite after the Proctor monumental division was shut down. (Courtesy of PFL/PHS.)

After World War I, the Proctor American Legionnaires built a skating rink south of Olympus Road. In this photograph three pairs of dancing skaters swirl around the freshly frozen surface before a large group of onlookers. (Courtesy of PFL/PHS.)

Local hockey players share the ice with daredevil skaters practicing their barrel jumps. One at right in mid-air clears three barrels at once. When this picture was taken, overhead lighting had been installed to permit day and night use of the rink. The Vermont Marble Company and Proctor organizations nurtured a safe and pleasant community life with gifts of public parks and recreational facilities. One pre–World War II site was the swimming pool, a natural pond a little south of the present Chatterton Park development. (Courtesy of PFL/PHS.)

Two

PLACES

This oldest known Pittsford glass plate image is of the old Otter Creek House. It was probably taken in 1848 by Frederic Edwin Church, an early camera enthusiast. His diary that year records staying at Rand's Tavern sketching Pittsford scenes. His signed and dated painting is of this view in every detail except for a horse and carriage in place of the man in the street. The brick store (left) still stands. (Author's collection.)

Otter Creek flows north for its entire length. In Florence, Stevens Brook flows in from the left, creating the sand spit named Pitt's Ford for William Pitt, the British friend of the American colonists. The remains of Roger Stevens Jr.'s 1775 gristmill are still on the brook, not far above the ford way. A Tory sympathizer, he moved to Canada after the Revolution.

The Otter Creek House was replaced by the Otter Creek Inn, shown here about 1895 in its heyday. Families from "away" spent whole summers here. The Browns and Armingtons from Providence, Rhode Island, escaped the heat while visiting Pittsford relatives and friends, as did the Walkers, Willards, and other New York City people with roots in Pittsford. An exception was Desmond Kelly—the red-haired New York actress arrived one summer accompanied by her very attentive agent, throwing Pittsford wives into anxious fits that their husbands would follow her back to the city. The inn burned in 1931.

This is an early-1900s village view of Ray and McCormick's brick store (left), built in 1838. Note the rail in front for tying horses. Store owner successors were William T. Denison and his son William E. Denison. Harold Phillips joined the latter in 1946. It continued in various commercial uses. Daniel and Judith Keith now own a sporting goods and screen print shop. Next to the store are William E. Denison's post office and home. At far right is the Old Hotel's livery stable, moved there in 1895 to make room to build the Walter Memorial Building, now Maclure Library. (Author's collection.)

Ice-coated elms line Elm Street in the winter of 1920. By the 1950s, every tree was dead or dying of Dutch elm disease and the inn was only a dim memory.

Dr. Henry Haven Swift's home and office on Elm Street, formerly Dr. A. M. Caverly's, once faced the inn where Kamuda's store is now. Swift married Caverly's daughter Caroline. The house was built by Stephen Avery in 1799. Caverly remodeled the exterior in the Italianate style. This is the same car seen behind him in the view of him setting up his camera. (Author's collection.)

The monument marking the site of Fort Vengeance on the stage road to Brandon was dedicated in 1873. The fort was barely finished in 1780 when Native Americans killed a soldier outside the gate. Maj. Ebenezer Allen smashed a bottle of rum on the gate to christen Fort Vengeance. A high palisade enclosed an acre of land around Deacon Caleb Hendee's buildings, which were converted to military uses.

The dam by the old Brown tannery pond, shop (left), and owner's house on the Rutland Road are intact in this 1921 image. The dam and shop are gone, but tanner and currier Elijah Brown's house remains. He came to Pittsford about 1783. He was related to the Providence, Rhode Island, Browns and Armingtons. (Author's collection.)

The East Pittsford Dam construction crew and seven teams of horses line up for a portrait in the basin formed while East Creek was diverted to a temporary channel prior to starting the new dam. (Courtesy of John and Linda Weeden.)

Looking from east to west, the East Pittsford Dam and fieldstone sidewalls laid up in cement begin to take shape. When finished they will all be sheathed with a relatively smooth exterior surface of the same materials. (Courtesy of John and Linda Weeden.)

William Eayres's early model of a power-driven corn chopper predates the current tractors pulling machines that cut corn in the field, chop it into finer ensilage than this old one did, blow it into a wagon behind it, and deliver the load to a free-standing silo instead of a barn loft above the cows. This barn was behind Sawdi's Restaurant, a bit north of the farmhouse on the Rutland Road. (Courtesy of Rebecca Degenhardt Mandolare.)

Richard (Dick) Mooney's family lived next door to John Matthews's family in this Granger company house on Furnace Road. Mooney was a moulder and boss in the foundry. Dick's son Patrick was born here in 1865. In the 1950s, he recorded his memories of going to work at age 14 at the Furnace after his father died. Patrick grew up to be a construction boss at Vermont Marble Company in charge of building several power dams in the Otter Creek valley and oversaw finishing the marble bridge in Proctor.

Behind these two houses on Cedar Street (Route 7 in Pittsford Village) stood Newton and Thompson's box factory. It shared the driveway with McCormick's livery stable. The sign is visible between the houses. Cedar Street was so named after Mary Jane Eaton planted a cedar hedge at the foot of Evergreen Cemetery in the distance. (Author's collection.)

This photograph shows Isaac's Leap as it cascades down the Haskins Brook from Chittenden past the Furnace in Grangerville. It was also called Manganese Brook because it originates near the beds of manganese added to Granger stoves to strengthen the metal and retard rusting. Swift's trademark habit of placing human figures in his compositions helps to gauge the falls' height. (Author's collection.)

This view west to the Taconics was taken from the Noyes sisters' house in the village. The fields are behind houses facing Route 7. Herrick Mountain shows faintly at the far left. The Pinckney (left) and Hutchinson houses were built in 1911 and 1908. The John Eayres house at far right was built in 1912 shortly before the picture was taken. The peaked mountain above this house is at the right of the mountain distinctively named Biddies Knob.

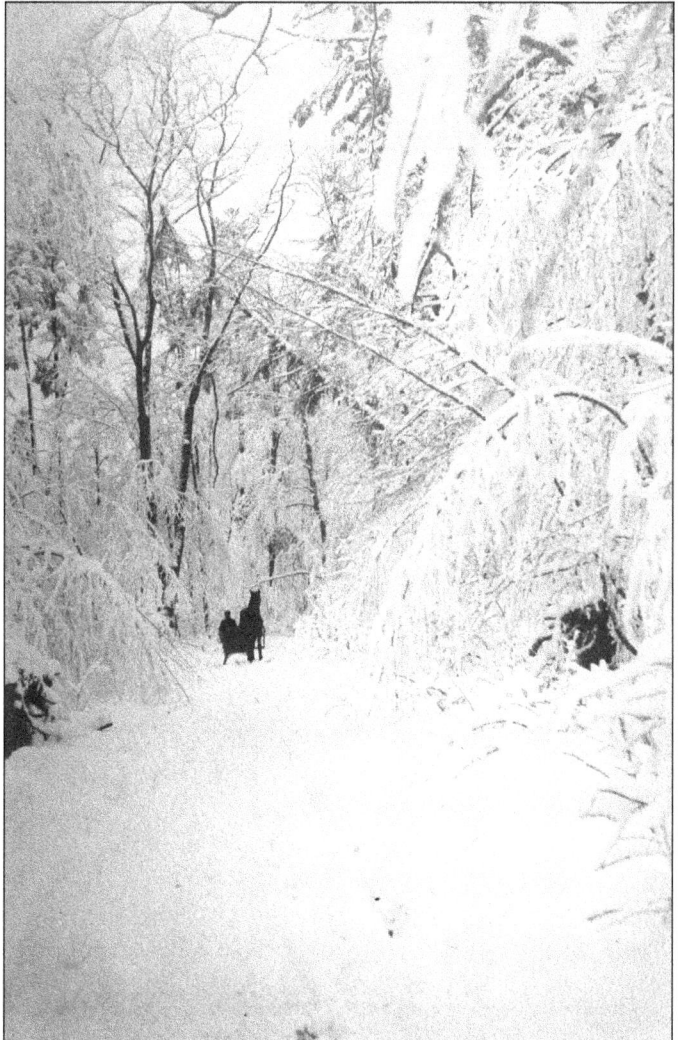

Sleighing in the Vermont Sanatorium woods was a favorite winter pastime. Redfield Proctor Sr. built "the San" with a farm and this pine forest in Pittsford for company workers and their tubercular spouses. A new wing added in 1930 treated patients with silicosis. The Proctors gave the property to the state in 1921 and built a separate facility for patients' children in 1923. With tuberculosis on the wane "the San" closed in 1966. It is now the Vermont Police and Fire Academy. (Author's collection.)

NICKWACKETT FARM, J.B. CANDON, PROP, PITTSFORD, VT. 1916.

Chittenden farmer John B. Candon bought this house and 80-acre Nickwackett Farm on the road to Brandon in 1899. He kept Jersey cows and made 300 pounds of butter from their cream every week. He also made ice cream and raised pigs and potatoes on the side. His dairy equipment, including the churns, was electrically driven. He was known as a very successful small farmer; his house was said to be furnished with Colonial furniture. Previous owner J. W. Willard Sr. raised champion Morgan horses.

Dr. Henry Haven Swift and Mary Randall Allen shot dozens of Pittsford views. This one looks northwest toward the village from Corn Hill Road. Cox Mountain (left) and Mount Nickwackett rise beyond the village. The year 1816 became "the Year of No Summer" when all gardens in town were repeatedly killed by frosts except for one cornfield just below this spot. Corn Hill has been named as such ever since. (Author's collection.)

The view east from West Road in Florence includes Pittsford Village with the Green Mountains behind. When settlers established Pittsford Village in 1774, it was covered with wild blackberry bushes and is still known as Blackberry Hill. In the foreground are large depressions left after excavating sand for Vermont Marble Company's gang saws in its Florence and Proctor mills.

This pre-1890 winter scene, looking northwest to Florence, was taken from John M. Goodnough's farm pasture in Pittsford Village. The slopes of flat-topped Biddies Knob and others in the Taconic range had begun to recover from being grazed bare by thousands of sheep in the 1850s. The future Florence marble mill and mill workers' homes would be built among the lowest foothills below the peaked mountain (center). (Author's collection.)

Dr. Henry Haven Swift's long view of Pittsford valley from Blueberry Hill is framed by the Taconics (left) and Cox Mountain. The pastures on Blueberry Hill and adjacent Sangamon Hill in the southeast part of town are now mostly grown over with woods interspersed with homes built after World War II. (Author's collection.)

In the late 1800s, the Slosson family fled New York City's summer heat for their brick house on Route 7 overlooking Pittsford Mills, at the south end of the village. This view west from their house includes St. Alphonsus Church and its gambrel-roofed parsonage. They stand out among homes, barns, and farm fields. Lumber mills, factories, William B. Shaw's store, and the Mills Bridge are just out of sight at left. (Author's collection.)

A postcard of the Mills Bridge dated 1914 reveals the automobile's impact on the landscape. Nicholas Powers's bridge over Furnace Brook, the bandstand, and the Rich house and post office (right) all disappeared in 1931 when Route 7 was paved with cement. At left is the Catholic church tower. William B. Shaw's brick store is behind the bandstand.

Pittsford Mills

William B. Shaw's store burned before the 1901 fire that destroyed every mill building and factory along Furnace Brook. His house (the former Penfield Tavern) was miraculously undamaged, considering that the town had but two horse-drawn hose carts. Shaw repaired the store to its present appearance. The house was demolished in 1997. Architectural fragments are in the historical society museum.

Town Hill Road runs west from Pittsford Village across Otter Valley to the ruins of the covered Mead Bridge over the creek. The bridge burned in 1971. This road connected the east branch of the Crown Point Military Road to the original route from Center Rutland through Proctor and Florence to Brandon.

The Mead Bridge survived the 1927 flood, but in William T. and Grace Davenport's house at the west end of the bridge the waters had risen over the piano keys in their living room before subsiding to the level shown here. The rowboat by their porch was their only means of transport for several days. (Courtesy of Rebecca Davenport.)

Pittsford native Dr. Henry Walker built the Walker Memorial Building for town offices and a library in the wye formed by Route 7 (left) and Arch Street (right) in 1895, dedicating it to the memory of his brother Stephen Walker, who designed the aqueduct system piping spring water from Mount Nickwackett to the village. The watering trough honors horse dealer John Goodnough, who raised funds for the aqueduct.

The 1835 Baptist church facing Plains Road in Pittsford Village burned in 1914. The first log meeting house stood on the site, serving Baptists and Congregationalists, and as a town hall. The steeple closely resembles that of the White Meeting House on the village green. It was moved aside in 1836 to make room for the present brick Congregational church.

Pittsford's railroad station was built in 1896 at the foot of Depot Hill. Fifty years later it was dismantled when rail officials suspended passenger service. Henry Kingman's horse and stage (left) are ready to take the mail up to the post office in Pittsford Village. Every morning a hired boy poured water over the wheels to swell the wood against the iron rims before the first mail run. Dr. John I. Pinckney's wife waits on the platform for a train. Her high-button blue shoes are in the historical society's museum. (Author's collection.)

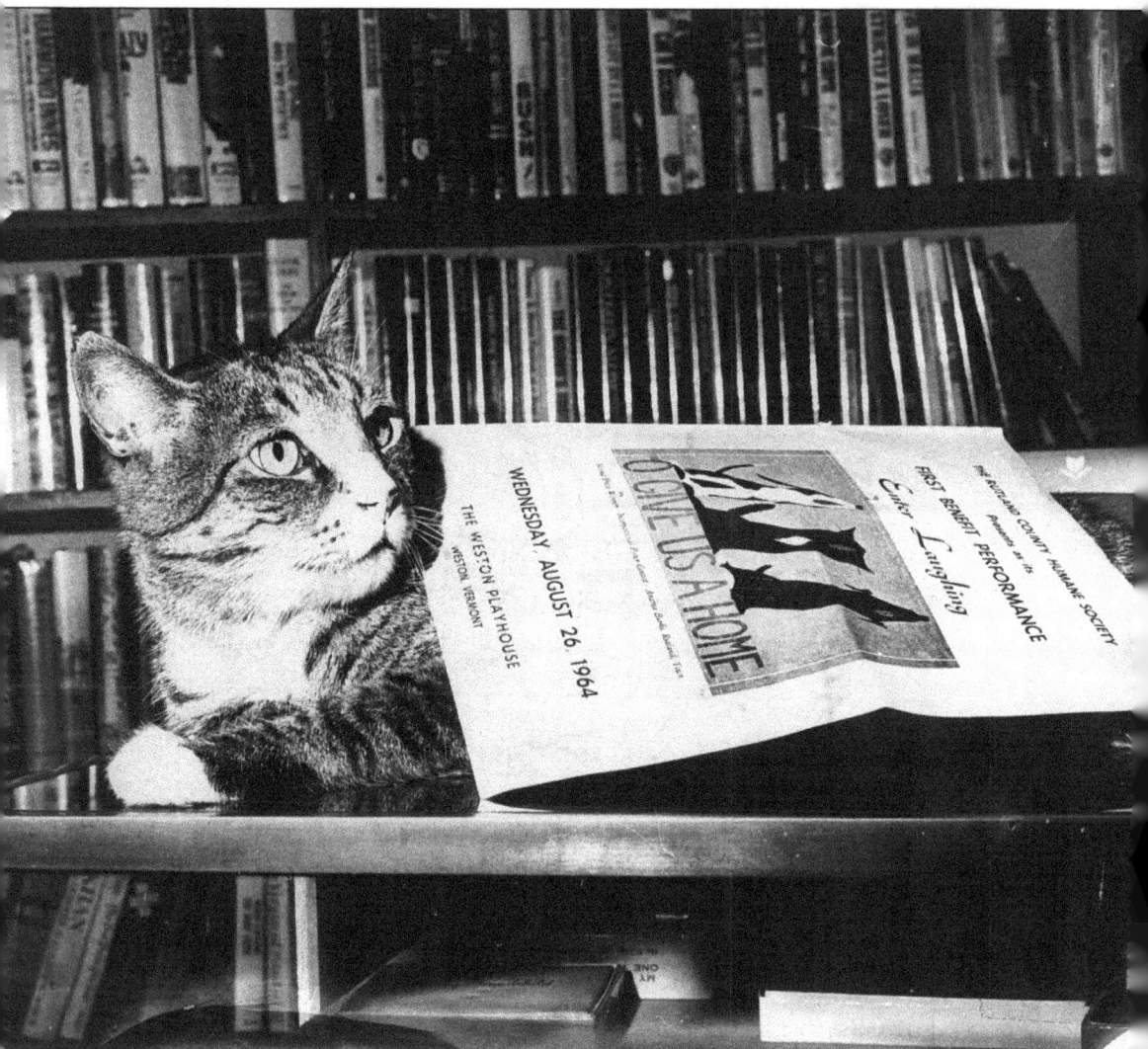

One of thousands of pet animals rescued and adopted since 1959, this cat represents the Rutland County Humane Society and founders Ellen Hollrock and Olive Smith of Rutland. Edward Wheeler was the first humane society agent; his Pittsford barn was the shelter until the new one on Stevens Road was built in 1967. The poster announces a benefit performance at the Weston Playhouse. (Courtesy of Beth Saradarian.)

Waterfalls were everywhere in Pittsford. Sugar Hollow Brook had at least four dams with mills, Furnace Brook had four, and there were two in Florence, along with Otter Creek's Sutherland Falls. Perley Kendrick and son Luke built this mill and dam on Sugar Hollow Brook in 1860. They and later owners cut and sold tons of ice into the 1930s. The person on the dam provides scale, a regular feature in Dr. Henry Haven Swift's scenes. (Author's collection.)

The deep hole above Furnace Brook has been a favorite fishing spot and swimming hole, but the stream's powerful current has claimed more than one life. Young Charles Smith died in 1927 of a skull fracture when he dove into the pool. Helen Howland died around 1950 when the car she was riding in plunged off Furnace Bridge into the frozen brook. Dr. H. L. Frost tried for hours, but could not revive her.

As pictured recently, the Granger house at Furnace Flat retains the original cast-iron window and door lintels. Simeon Granger and Sons produced cast-iron stoves in the 1840s and shipped them throughout the Northeast. They employed 50 or more men who lived close by in company-owned houses. The house, now a bed-and-breakfast, looks across Furnace Road to the remains of the blast furnace's stone stack that was over 50 feet tall when built. Israel Keith built the first furnace on this land in 1791.

Edward Smith was bookkeeper at the Furnace before it closed in the 1880s. Smith earned extra income by making fly and bait fishing rods of bamboo and other exotic woods in this shop on Furnace Road. Most sold for $7.50 with two tips, a reel seat, and cloth bag. His ledger lists clients from all over North America.

Partway up Furnace Hill above the Granger house the Barnard Road veers right and passes the old Raymond Barnard farm before ending at German Hill between Holden and South Chittenden. This view of the roadster and Barnard house dates from about 1930. The exterior has hardly changed, but present owners Louis and Nancy Gaudreau have rearranged the interior. (Courtesy of Barbara Ketcham.)

Leone Smith (left) and two helpers gather sap from Camp Sangamon's maples on the farm they bought on Jackson Hill (now Sangamon Hill) around 1920. Except for the sugar bush the hilltop around the original house, now the camp lodge, was largely bare of trees but is now grown up to relatively young woods. (Courtesy of Camp Sangamon.)

Girls at Camp Betsey Cox thrive in the fresh air and mountain scenery shown here. For the camp's first season co-owner Charles Davies built two rustic cabins—Killington and Mansfield—with canvas bunks for the girls. He added fieldstone fireplaces before the second season opened. Boys and girls swim and boat at Burr Pond below the camps. (Courtesy of Camp Betsey Cox.)

Sangamon Road runs down past the upper end of the reservoir created by Central Vermont Public Service's East Pittsford Dam. Dr. Henry Haven Swift titled this 1900s view "Spirit Vale, East Pittsford," perhaps alluding to the Eddy family of spiritualists whose land bordered the pond. Days and nights of heavy rain in 1947 broke the dam, leaving cottages and docks along the banks high and dry. The damage downstream to Rutland Town and Rutland City was enormous. (Author's collection.)

This early-1900s view from the east end of the unfinished "Little Dam" shows, from left to right, the Osgood barns (now Jay Newton's), Nina Brush's house and barn (now Michael Nesshoever's), John and Linda Weeden's home since 1965, East Pittsford Cemetery, and the Methodist Episcopal church and sheds. (Courtesy of John and Linda Weeden.)

This chore had to be done before the pond could be filled. An unusual front-end mowing machine cuts hay planted while East Creek was diverted from its natural channel. The horse at right powers a catapult as two men fork hay into giant piles. (Courtesy of John and Linda Weeden.)

Dan Rollins and a Mr. Emerson stand on a portable sawmill behind a four-horse team in South Chittenden. The house is part of the Osgood farm now owned by Jay Newton. (Courtesy of CHS.)

Central Vermont Public Service's "Big Dam" in Chittenden was completed in 1900. Surrounded by the Green Mountain National Forest, the reservoir covers 17 square miles. Arthur Wardwell recalls that it took just 12 days to fill. Mount Carmel (center) rises above the north end with Bloodroot Mountain at far left. In 1947, water poured over the dam, causing the rampaging East Creek to destroy buildings and the bridge in South Chittenden. (Courtesy of John and Linda Weeden.)

Dr. Henry Haven Swift caught trout for breakfast from the porch of his camp in Chittenden. Swift's first camp was a huge canvas tarpaulin stretched taut over a pole. A dozen people could—and did—cook, sew, read, play games, and sleep under it. Swift spent summers at camp while his associate doctors cared for patients in Pittsford Village. (Author's collection.)

Hikers like the great views southwest from Mount Nickwackett in Chittenden. Swift's title, "Near the Sand Spring, where we get our water," identifies the source of Pittsford's water supply since 1895. The buildings are Robert and Bonnie Baird's farm on West Road. They own over 600 acres of woods and fields, much of them protected by the Vermont Land Trust. (Author's collection.)

A hip-booted fisherman casts into the waters by Cheedle's mill that overhung Furnace Brook in Holden around 1900. Timothy Cheedle's house is above the dam. Joseph Howard owned the place in the mid-1900s. Lumber baron C. Reed Holden bought this mill and eventually owned all the sawmills in town. Later he bought the Goodnough/Pinckney house in Pittsford Village and moved there in 1917. He built the small barn behind the house. (Author's collection.)

Above Holden village, Dr. Margaret Waddington spends the year writing her books at Furnace Brook Farm, the Morgan horse farm formerly owned by Dr. Frank and Margaret Lathrop. Waddington and her friend and neighbor Katherine Sivret keep the fields and pastures open with two tractor mowers and tend the flower beds and berry bushes. (Courtesy of Dr. Waddington.)

Above the Waddington farm is one of Chittenden's geological curiosities, variously called Chimney Rock, Sentinel Rock, and the Pulpit. Old men remember scaling it to the very top when they were boys being challenged by their daring young friends.

This old car appears to have stalled while turning off Barnard Road onto German Hill above Holden village. Barnard Road used to cross here and continue over the mountain ridge into Pittsfield. The old Elliott farm is visible at the foot of the hill. The house was damaged by fire years ago, and all the original farm buildings have since disappeared. (Author's collection.)

Judge Edwin Horton's residence (right) in South Chittenden is shown on the road to what is now Mountain Top Inn and Resort. (In 1869, it was the Henry Long farm.) Long turned 90 in 1926, and Horton was 85. The Chittenden Reservoir, far below the inn, provides a magnificent view and swimming beach for guests of the year-round inn. (Courtesy of CHS.)

Sutherland Falls were so named for John Sutherland when they were located in the south part of Pittsford. After the town of Proctor was created in 1887, the falls were in Proctor. The dam and powerhouse above them still supply power to the town at very favorable rates. The Swinging Bridge used to be a shortcut for Patch Hill residents to walk across the falls. It was taken down in the 1940s. (Author's collection.)

This northerly view in Dr. Henry Haven Swift's album, taken from the top of the falls, is titled "The Meadows at High Tide." The floodwaters to the right of the island (center) roughly outline the beaver pond that first settler Gideon Cooley drained for his own use in 1769. Cox Mountain and Mount Nickwackett (right) form the backdrop. (Author's collection.)

Around 1895, Jessie Warner Eckley took this view of the covered bridge above the falls from her lawn. Her grandfather Myron C. Warner tore down John Sutherland's decrepit house and built his own on the same foundation in 1872. Warner's son-in-law F. S. Eckley (Jessie's father) owned it when this image was taken. (Courtesy of SLD.)

This view of the marble span that replaced the wooden one in 1915 shows how Main Street's westerly approach to the bridge was raised, much to the annoyance of the Eckleys. However, they improved the yard with flower beds, shrubbery, and an attractive fence that afforded more privacy and reduced the sound of traffic. (Courtesy of SLD.)

At the top of East Street, above the marble bridge, once stood this small house owned by the Ormsbee family. It was there in 1890 but gone by the time the present Proctor Free Library was erected nearer to the bridge in 1913. This photograph was found in Jessie Eckley's collection. (Courtesy of SLD.)

The Warner/Eckley house is pictured facing Main Street on February 10, 1896, before the road was raised. Otter Creek is just out of sight at left. In another picture of the house in the 1927 flood the creek had risen high enough to cover the first-floor windowsills. The street on Powers Hill was also completely washed down into Meadow Street, leaving houses dangling over the chasm. (Courtesy of SLD.)

The 1927 flood devastated the area around the marble company yards. A boxcar washed off its track is pinned against the station. The 1836 stone school building and Vermont Marble Company's new office building (left) appear to have escaped flooding. The office building replaced the old one near the station. (Courtesy of SLD.)

Frank Samuel Eckley owned and operated this store on the same side of the railroad bridge as his house. The Eckley property was purchased by Herbert Johnson Sr. in 1961 after being vacant and overgrown with wild berries for many years, according to Johnson's daughter Helen Johnson Newton, who lives there now. (Courtesy of SLD.)

Fred Warner's general store was on the north end of West Street. The West Street Market now occupies Warner's lot. Present owner David Atherton's research reveals that his brick store was built in 1930 by David W. McGarry. The poured foundation may be the first one in Proctor. McGarry was succeeded by storekeepers Frank LaPenna, Andrew Cristelli, and Atherton. (Courtesy of SLD.)

A massive ledge that became the Sutherland Falls quarry opened in 1838 and soon proved to be a major success. This view of the south face dates from around 1895. Located northwest of the intersection of Market and Main Streets, the quarry is abandoned and filled with water. It has become a quiet place for people to walk their dogs. (Author's collection.)

The houses of two members of the Proctor family have unfortunately disappeared from the landscape. Sen. Redfield Proctor built this house on the high promontory above Otter Creek, with the creek on one side and the railway station on the other. Surely he would enjoy the north view from the back porch over Sutherland Falls to Pittsford Village as well as that west to the marble works and park. Presidents Benjamin Harrison, William McKinley, and Theodore Roosevelt were his houseguests when they visited Proctor. (Courtesy of SLD.)

The arched paths to Sen. Redfield Proctor's front garden were decorated to welcome one of three U.S. presidents who were guests between 1891 and 1901. Power lines overhead suggest that the honored guest was Theodore Roosevelt in 1901. (Courtesy of PFL/PHS.)

This was the home of Senator Proctor's son Fletcher Proctor. It is a fine example of the Queen Anne style, with its delicate ornamentation and abundant windows letting in air and sunlight. It stood on a rise above South Street diagonally opposite the future site of the Proctor Free Library. (Courtesy of PFL/PHS.)

The first hospital was built in 1896 for Vermont Marble Company employees and their families. It stood on the west side of South Street. Dr. Henry Haven Swift saved the life of a Florence man whose arm was mangled by machinery in the Center Rutland mill. The *Rutland Herald* reported a week later that the man's arm had to be amputated but he was recovering nicely. After the second hospital opened, this one was greatly expanded to become the Marble Town Inn. It has since gone the way of many structures: destroyed instead of undergoing adaptive rehabilitation for new uses. (Courtesy of PFL/PHS.)

This second hospital was on Ormsbee Avenue. The gray marble wing as well as the new obstetrics wing to the south were added later before it closed for good and was torn down. Doctors and surgeons practicing here included, among others, Dr. Henry Fregosi and Dr. Albert Fregosi, Dr. Harry Ryan of Rutland, and Dr. Henry Haven Swift of Pittsford. (Courtesy of PFL/PHS.)

In Proctor's downtown, this small stone building on the west side of the park started life in 1836 as the first school in town. It housed the third town library from 1891 to 1913 and was converted to its present use as the town offices on the ground level with a meeting room and office upstairs. It is one of the few buildings facing the park to escape demolition. (Courtesy of SLD.)

The little pines suggest that the town park was completed shortly before the picture was taken. The tower of the second Union Church (built in 1891 after the first one burned) rises above the 1866 stone building, which was the second school. The marble-trimmed commercial building (right) was called the Real Estate Building because Forrest Thomas's real estate office was on the second floor with Florence Mead's music studio and Dr. George Somers's dental offices. Dances and other large gatherings were held on the top floor. After it was torn down the lot was left vacant. Partially hidden by a tree is the much-loved town hall. (Courtesy of PFL/PHS.)

The Real Estate Building (left) overlooks the park and bandstand to the marble mills and yards with Mount Nickwackett beyond. The rubble in the foreground was left from the demolition of the old stone school in 1914 to make room for the new Cooperative Company Store between the Real Estate Building and Church Street. (Courtesy of PFL/PHS.)

The temperature was four degrees below zero when this image was made of the Real Estate Building under construction. The town hall (center) was later doomed to destruction and replaced by the recently completed fire station, appropriately finished with marble tiles. The old YMCA building (right) was destined to become the Sutherland Club. (Courtesy of SLD.)

One of many outcroppings in Proctor looms over buildings that still stand at the corner of Market Street and School Street. The Proctor Gas Company office currently occupies the site. The profile of a Native American's head in the rock at left is still faintly discernible. (Author's collection.)

St. Dominic's Catholic Church (1880–1926) stood facing North Street at the top of Powers Hill. This church and the first Union Church, with similar steeples, strongly resembled each other. This building and the North Street School (left) were in the vee formed by North Street and the Florence Road. The school is still there, but it was turned to face the Florence Road before being converted to a residence. The marble retaining wall in the foreground ran along North Street and partway down Powers Hill. (Courtesy of SLD.)

In the 1880s, Dr. John Johnson contracted to have built for him the eclectic brick castle and matching outbuildings still to be seen near the southern end of West Street (also known as West Proctor Road). George D. Bates of Pittsford laid the parquet floors. Furnishings include the lamp with a Tiffany glass shade hanging above the table in this view of the library. Now named Wilson Castle, it is open to the public during the summer and fall. (Courtesy of PFL/PHS.)

Immigrant marble workers built the Greek Catholic church in 1906 on a little rise above East Street in Proctor. Its title on this postcard, "Ruska Cerkov," lends a hint of an eastern European language. It was later referred to as the Greek Orthodox church. It was an Independent Christian Chapel in 1937. The steeple is gone, and now it is a Masonic lodge. (Courtesy of PFL/PHS.)

Among other events, Proctor gardeners held flower shows in the town hall. In this exhibit, whole trees and bushes surround the floral arrangements, and the balcony is draped in greens. The flowers stand out against the hall's dark stained woodwork. People still bemoan the demolition of this landmark building. (Courtesy of PFL/PHS.)

Three

PRODUCTS

Samuel Crippen built the first dam and gristmill on Sugar Hollow Brook above Colburn Bridge in Pittsford Village in 1772. After their first building at the Furnace burned in 1904, Newton and Thompson moved their box factory to this site. Some 50 men and women made lathe-turned pillboxes, billy clubs, bowling pins, toys, and baseball bats. Wooden mailboxes were another big item. Arthur Wardwell from Chittenden worked here around the time he was a student at the nearby high school.

About 25 feet of stones had been removed from the top of the Granger blast furnace stack for other uses when this picture was taken around 60 years ago. Iron ore was mixed with charcoal and a limestone flux to produce molten iron that flowed from the arch into beds of sand divided into "pigs," thereby explaining the term *pig iron*.

The Florence-Fowler marble mill built in 1898 was once the second longest in the world. The stack was 125 feet tall. Rough stock was the first product, but monumental quality was soon added in the finishing shop. Beginning pay was 7.5¢ an hour for 10 hours a day, six days a week. Everyone shopped at the company store and lived in company-owned houses or boardinghouses. Only the stack and a few houses remain now. (Author's collection.)

Pittsford marble was mostly white, cloud-gray, or blue-gray. From the time a few private quarries opened in Florence, marble was the choice for foundations, door and window lintels, and cemetery stones. This one in the Congregational cemetery honors Jeremiah Powers, who died in 1801. His grandson Nicholas M. Powers was a famed covered bridge builder. Powers Hill in Proctor is named for this family. (Author's collection.)

Benjamin Nixon's chair factory was powered by this dam on Sugar Hollow Brook in the village. His hardwood straight chairs had turned legs and splint seats. Some had arms. Some were stained a soft brick red, but most were painted black with narrow yellow ochre striping or stenciled back splats. All weighed very little. William Cotting succeeded Nixon in the business in the 1860s. (Author's collection.)

One of Dr. Henry Haven Swift's patients was Grace Woolson. Although her health was fragile, she had a strong will and wrote the authoritative book on ferns native to Vermont, *Ferns and How to Grow Them*, published in 1914 by Doubleday Page and Company. The illustrations are Swift's photographs. This lacy little wall rue is one of some 50 fern species found in and around Pittsford. (Author's collection.)

This handsome cast-iron parlor stove is an example of hundreds of stoves moulded in the Granger foundry. Highly skilled pattern makers designed many more models in the Granger era from 1826 to 1852. The stoves had one thing in common: their removable legs were all identical. Pancake griddles, door latches and hinges, and window weights were among other products of the foundry.

Low-quality marble was seldom wasted. These chunks of discarded stone shored up the Adams Road in Pittsford around 1900. Gravestones either damaged or with incorrect data were uncovered in the abutments of the Gorham Bridge that connects Pittsford to Proctor during major structural repairs a few years ago.

The marble slabs waiting to be laid for a sidewalk through Pittsford Village were a product of the Vermont Marble Company mills in Proctor. John W. Willard and his springer spaniel are seated in front of the Otter Creek Inn about 1888. He was one of three inventors whose patented stamp-vending machine was in the inn's lobby. It probably burned with the inn in 1931.

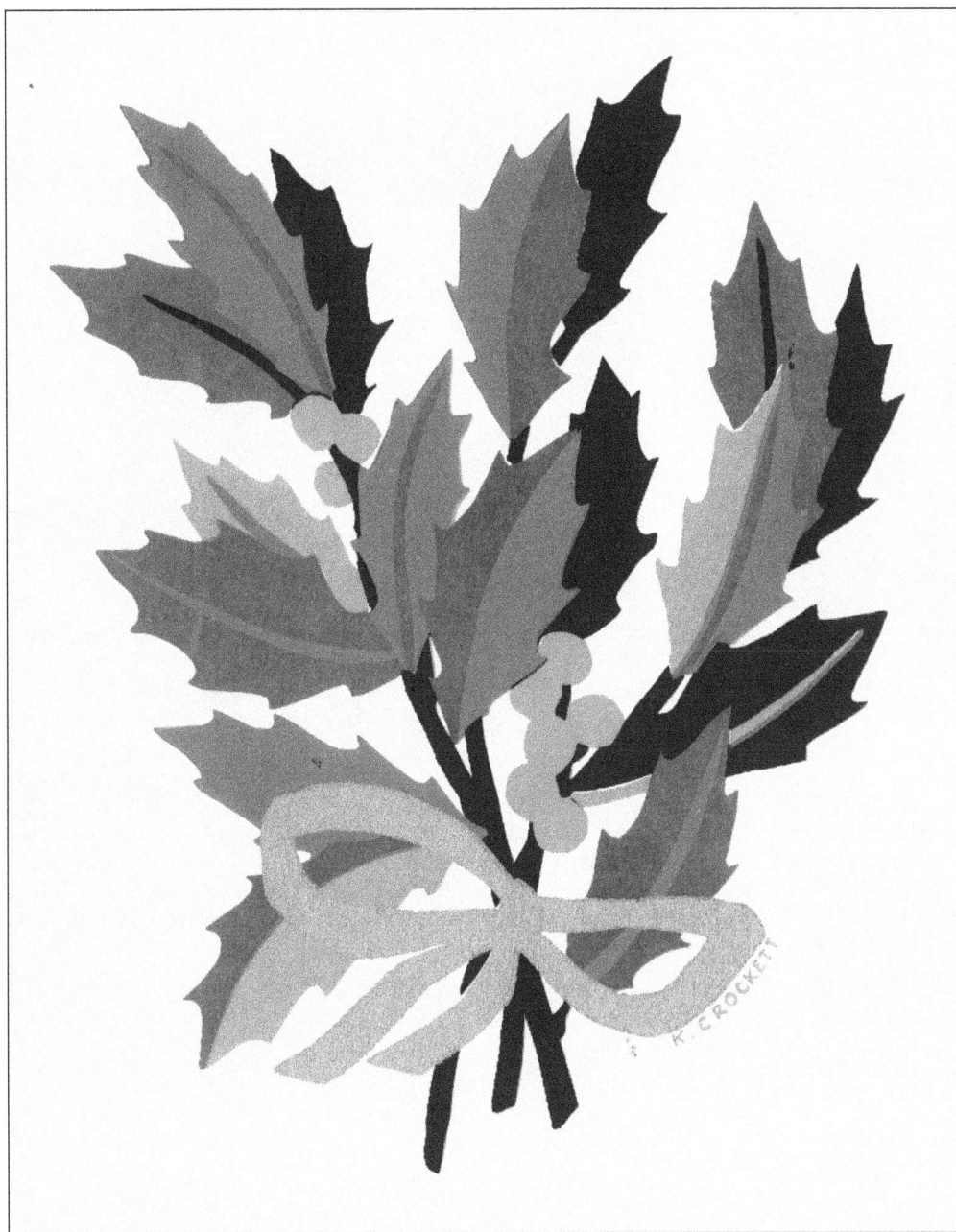

Katherine Crockett started in business with handmade silk-screened cards in New York City. In 1947, she bought the Sturtevant barns on Furnace Road for her studio and living quarters. She kept six local women busy printing and shipping enough cards every year to move the post office's category to the next level. She retired and sold the business in 1965. This is one of her own distinctive designs. By overprinting transparent colors, she achieved three shades of green, with a scarlet bow. (Author's collection.)

At the Baird Farm in Chittenden, Bonnie Baird (center) and two beekeeping friends set up two new beehives on a flat shed roof, with a clover field already planted down below for the bees. The dark roof warmed them sooner in the spring, and the handy food supply resulted in 300 to 400 pounds of honey per year from just two hives. (Courtesy of Robert and Bonnie Baird.)

The products of Chittenden's great numbers of sawmills, clapboard mills, and blacksmith shops are next to impossible to illustrate photographically at this late date. The same is true for the tons of iron ore, charcoal, and manganese produced for the Pittsford furnace, and the carloads of potatoes shipped out of the Pittsford depot. Apparently they were never captured on film. This lone image of an unidentified Chittenden driver with a wagonload of planks drawn by two horses must serve to illustrate the town's primary industry since it was founded in 1780. The curious device atop the planks may have helped in lifting them onto the wagon. (Courtesy of CHS.)

This photograph of a giant overhead crane was among Jessie Eckley's collection. The scene is a Vermont Marble Company block pile near Beaver Pond in Proctor. The crane dwarfs the three men at the foot of its right base. In one of the mill buildings next to the park, the Vermont Marble Exhibit displays marble from quarries once owned by the company as well as marble jewelry, rolling pins, cheese boards, bookends, and more household items. (Courtesy of SLD.)

BIBLIOGRAPHY

Caverly, A. M., M.D. *History of the Town of Pittsford, VT.* Rutland, VT: Tuttle and Company, Printers, 1872.

Gale, David C. *Proctor, The Story of A Marble Town.* Brattleboro, VT: The Vermont Printing Company, 1922.

Pittsford Historical Society Inc. *Pittsford's Second Century, 1872–1997.* West Kennebunk, Maine: Phoenix Publishing, 1998.

Proctor Historical Society. *Proctor—The Way It Was.* Poultney, VT: Journal Press, Inc., 1975.

Woolson, Grace. *Ferns and How to Grow Them.* New York: Doubleday, Page and Company, 1914.

Visit us at
arcadiapublishing.com